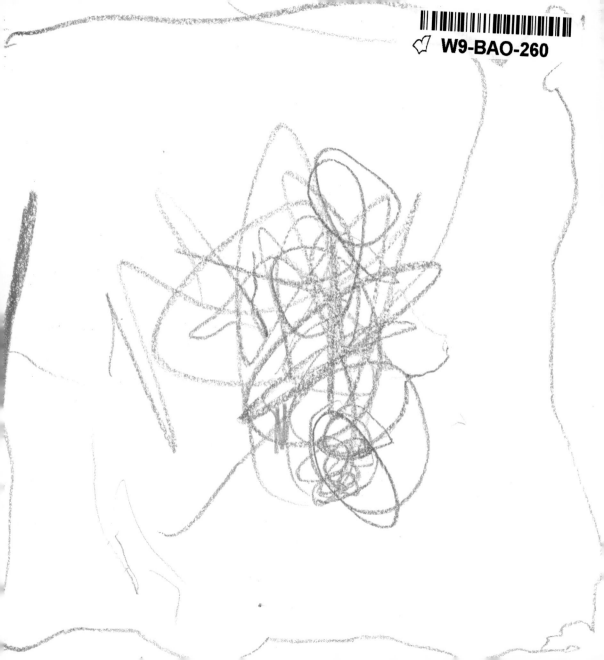

Animals in the Field

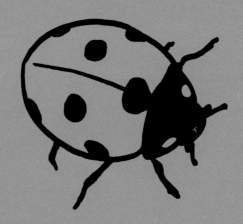

Élisabeth de Lambilly-Bresson

GARETH**STEVENS**

GS PUBLISHING

A Member of the WRC Media Family of Companies

The Hare

I am a hare.
I look like a rabbit,
but I have much longer ears.
My strong legs
are made for jumping.
When I run a race with rabbits,
I always come in first.

The Mole

I am a mole.
I dig tunnels underground
and hardly ever stop to rest.
I do not mind
that I am almost blind
because I am always
in the dark.

The Snail

I am a snail.
I carry my house on my back
so I am always at home!
When I get tired
of sliding across the fields,
I just stop where I am
and tuck myself
inside my shell to sleep.

The Magpie

I am a magpie.
I am a big, noisy bird.
I am also a thief!
I steal other birds' eggs.
I love to take things that glitter,
sparkle, and shine.
So hide your shiny toys!

The Bee

I am a bee.
I gather sweet nectar from
flowers in gardens and fields.
I make honey in my hive.
Would you like to taste some?

The Ladybug

I am a ladybug.
You might find me walking
along a blade of grass,
but I can fly, too.
If I land on you, I might walk
up your arm and tickle you
with my tiny feet.

The Butterfly

I am a butterfly.
My colorful wings make me
look like a flying flower.
I float from blossom
to blossom,
drinking sweet nectar.
Please do not catch me
in your butterfly net!

Please visit our Web site at: www.garethstevens.com
For a free color catalog describing Gareth Stevens Publishing's
list of high-quality books and multimedia programs, call
1-800-542-2595 (USA) or 1-800-387-3178 (Canada).
Gareth Stevens Publishing's fax: (414) 332-3567.

Library of Congress Cataloging-in-Publication Data

Lambilly-Bresson, Elisabeth de.
    [Dans les champs. English]
    Animals in the field / Elisabeth de Lambilly-Bresson. — North American ed.
        p. cm. — (Animal show and tell)
    ISBN-13: 978-0-8368-7831-8 (lib. bdg.)
    1. Meadow animals—Juvenile literature. I. Title.
    QL115.5L3613   2007
    591.74'6—dc22   2006032929

This edition first published in 2007 by
Gareth Stevens Publishing
A Member of the WRC Media Family of Companies
330 West Olive Street, Suite 100
Milwaukee, WI 53212 USA

Translation: Gini Holland
Gareth Stevens editor: Gini Holland
Gareth Stevens art direction and design: Tammy West

This edition copyright © 2007 by Gareth Stevens, Inc. Original edition copyright © 2002 by
Mango Jeunesse Press. First published as *Les animinis: Dans les champs* by Mango Jeunesse Press.

Printed in the United States of America

1 2 3 4 5 6 7 8 9 10 10 09 08 07 06